BROKEN
CONSCIOUSNESS

D1269511

BROKEN
CONSCIOUSNESS

Reflections of an Epileptic

Maggie Mendus

*For my lovely friend
Isabel
Love,
Maggie*

iUniverse, Inc.
Bloomington

Broken Consciousness
Reflections of an Epileptic

iUniverse books may be ordered through booksellers or by contacting:

iUniverse
1663 Liberty Drive
Bloomington, IN 47403
www.iuniverse.com
1-800-Authors (1-800-288-4677)

ISBN: 978-1-4620-0179-8 (pbk)
ISBN: 978-1-4620-0180-4 (ebk)

Printed in the United States of America

iUniverse rev. date: 3/31/2011

To my husband Michael, steady and strong,
my children, Molly and Christopher, understanding and sweet,
my mother, who gave me her heart,
my father, who opened the door to words,
my brother Tom, honest and humorous,
and my dear grandchildren, who provide the delight,

I love and thank you all.

Acknowledgments

I wish to express special thanks to my friend and fellow writer, Mariana Damon, for her long hours of listening and recommending. She invested herself in my work as if it were her own, and her encouragement always pointed me in the direction of more polished writing. I am also privileged to have known her husband, John Damon, who was a professor of medieval literature at the University of Nebraska at Kearney as well as an accomplished poet. His interest in my poetry was a compliment which I will remember with fondness.

Foreword

As one of the three million people in the United States suffering with epilepsy, I know firsthand what it's like to be laid low by a seizure. I remember the twelve year-old me, the frightened and confused child who woke up in the hospital not knowing what had happened to her.

"It was a convulsion, honey. You've had a convulsion."

I didn't even know where I was until I heard my mother's voice and noticed the unfamiliar surroundings. Bewildered, I didn't know what a convulsion was, nor did I much care. My head throbbed as if it had been stabbed. My doctor and some nurses clustered around my bed, happy that I was finally awake.

I had been diagnosed with the Asian flu, which affected a good portion of the U.S. population in 1957. I was twelve years old, and had been hospitalized for a week because of a fever of 105 that was associated with that flu. Soon an EEG confirmed that I also had epilepsy. No one else in my family had it, and I was placed on an anticonvulsant medication.

Despite the medicine, seizures occurred without warning. A typical seizure began with a period of time during which I would repeat myself many times over without making sense. An overwhelming fatigue along with disorientation combined with a loss of judgment and a blurred sense of my surroundings. A peculiar feeling overcame me which I was unable to explain to anyone. I became more and more distant, falling into a place where I could reach no one. A shriek signaled the beginning of the seizure when my arms and legs stiffened before the thrashing wracked my body.

During my career as an elementary and middle school teacher, having observed seizures in students, I knew only too well the fear, shame and depression they were experiencing. I, myself, had arrived at school in a compromised state more times than I care to count, having driven there unaware that I should never have placed myself behind the wheel. In every instance I was cared for in privacy in protection of my dignity, as a seizure, should one occur, is alarming to see.

The first medication I took caused depression so I was switched to another. When that did not lessen the incidence of seizure, another was added. I discovered that being epileptic meant having to maintain a continuous balancing act: Would swallowing an aspirin cause a seizure? Would cough medicine bring on the dreaded symptoms? Was a prescription for ciprofloxacin safe? Going to the drugstore began to assume frightening proportions. I had to carefully weigh and measure the consequences of taking even the most benign medications. Like a high-wire artist stepping gingerly across a tightrope, I couldn't afford a misstep.

My main seizure trigger is lack of sleep, and I have had to experiment with what that means. I am at my best after nine or ten hours of sleep at night. Caffeine and alcohol, even a cup of caffeinated tea or a glass of chardonnay, have had to be eliminated. Managing stress is crucial.

I am blessed to be married to a man who has educated himself about epilepsy and knows what to do in the event of a seizure. Through experience, he has learned how to deal with ambulance and emergency room personnel, who, unfortunately, are not always sympathetic to, or cooperative with, what I need.

I wish this burden had never fallen upon my husband and our children. At young ages, our daughter and son knew to call their grandma when Mom didn't seem just right. For 54 years epilepsy has dogged me, but within that time I have had long periods of being seizure-free. One of those was for 20 years, but as my mother lay dying, the stress of that time caused a breakthrough seizure, which seemed to open the door to more. As of this writing, I have been seizure-free for five years, one month and twenty-seven days. Yet the prospect of another looms like a dark cloud on the horizon.

Not being able to trust my brain is frustrating, and there are times when I feel that it has deserted me. Therefore, each day I wake up alert and with no signs of seizure I consider as a gift. Something we epileptics the world over share is a common sense of fragility and the common feeling of doom averted.

Maggie Mendus
February, 2011

Contents

Part One:
AURA

Understanding

Have you had thoughts that fade, then disappear
into the vapor of the atmosphere?
Have you awakened in a cloud of haze,
bumping the winding walls within a maze?
Have you been questioned, commonplace the task,
not knowing the answers to what they ask?
Have you lost days that cannot be retrieved,
days locked in silent absence, stolen, thieved?
Have you attempted normalcy but failed,
like a train that jumped the track, a train derailed?
If so, you may be seizure's captive too,
subdued by epilepsy's practiced crew.

Down the Rabbit Hole

I wasn't even peering down the hole
when something slugged me and I disappeared.
Now soundless are the songs of oriole.
I wasn't even peering down the hole.
Scratching the starless night for some control,
I cringe at dancing demons chandeliered.
I wasn't even peering down the hole
when something slugged me, and I disappeared.

Aura

Mountainous lands go flat. Lush landscapes blur
into unusual discomfiture.
Severe erosion scrapes the screaming shore
as unexpected thieves sneak in the door.
My mental fireplace logs burn down to ash
while neurons party in my brain. Their flash
eclipses power, and clouds fall from the sky,
a canopy I can't identify.
Ten clenching, frozen fingers clutch my head.
I try to steady drunken gait. Instead,
control just falls away. I fail, deny
the coming storm. I want to occupy
my world with quiet, but a maniac
grabs me with muscled arms of angry black.

The Beginning

When epilepsy kicked me in the teeth
I hadn't even reached my teenage years.
It threw me from the top of life beneath

to where the ocean waves originate.
The undertow enveloped me and stole
my fun-filled days, tried to eradicate

their festival. I fell before a fiend,
as if I had a choice. The confluence
of sunrise light and midnight dark careened

like screeching cars on some collision course.
With battle lines of grand mal seizure drawn,
the foe beleaguered me without remorse.

I fade away, diminish and decline,
my rigid arms and legs begin to thrash.
Three horrifying minutes pass. Supine

I stay for days, completely unaware.
When neurons start to scramble, I awake,
feel throbbing in my head. NO! Don't you dare!

Epilepsy through my Mind

The seizured mind stays hidden in thick cloaks,
averts its eyes to normal life, is flawed
like clocks whose hands won't move. As still as oaks,
the seizured mind stays hidden in thick cloaks.
I long for life without these heartless jokes
and grieve for all that now has been outlawed.
The seizured mind stays hidden in thick cloaks,
averts its eyes to normal life, is flawed.

Vacancy

What once made sense makes none right now.
I fight for reason, can't find how
to think the answers, battle tears,
pluck out the roots of all the fears
that threaten me. My brain feels cold,
summer fruit spoiling under mold.
I, stomping angry, strike the pose
of one whose whole world's doors now close,
and beg, "Please hear me, and extend
your hand. I'm disappearing, friend."

Surprise Attack

The biting jaws of seizure clamp again.
I fall into those biting jaws again.
Of darkness I become a denizen,

lose consciousness and disappear. Oh why,
my precious insights, do you vanish? Why?
How difficult I find it to apply

forgiveness to the mighty monsters there.
Forgiveness? To the mighty monsters? There
they work to leave my seizured mind threadbare.

Straight stitches are removed, fingers precise.
My mind's embroidery, once tight, precise,
hangs loose, an unstrung suture. When will splice

of hemispheres release me back to life?
Start knotting, please, and put away the knife.

Neurological Examination

"Close eyes, touch finger to your nose – again.
Turn hands palms up, palms down upon your knees."
Commands to follow, dolphin regimen
rule out the serious. This is a breeze.

"Get up and walk to let me check your gait."
Oh, I do this especially well.
Pupils reactive, reflexes just great.
This information and the facts now tell

that search is narrowed, the worst far out of reach.
"What is your name? What day is it?" I bow
my head in shame. These questionings impeach
intelligence. I hope he knows just how.

When all is done, results come to the fore:
"New symptoms have emerged we can't ignore."

Again

Again my weary brain falls off its perch,
swerves left while trying to avoid a lurch
into the odd abyss. Sea monsters wait
again to swallow me, to lacerate
the stitches very recently tied tight.
Must I again descend into this night?
What circumstances will at last combine
to change infected trees to fragrant pine?
Again I recognize the weird descent.
No matter how I voice my argument,
the engine steams along its cold, steel track
in greedy preparation to attack.

Part Two:
SEIZURE

Kindred

I share this trail of tears, this lineage
of famous and plain Jane. The thread that weaves
us like old brothers pillages like thieves.
We totter in the shadows on the bridge.

An emptying, like coins from neural bank,
abandons me to lands of poverty.
Through my trashed brain, once-capable, I see
debris. Again I have been shot point-blank.

And like that dead man, still, so still I lie
while each piece of my mind fights for its place.
Is agony apparent on my face?
What does this epilepsy signify?

I cannot capture those electric waves
that surge without control when seizures strike.
Inside my head I feel the sharpened spike.
I want to throw this chaos into graves.

The thuds continue. I find no escape.
Beneath their heavy hand I acquiesce
as sunset gold and pink turn colorless.
My mental landscapes flatten and change shape.

Fear screams that this could be a permanent
condition, and that narrowness defines
closed doors that once swung wide. Those deep gold mines,
instead, hold thicknesses of gray cement.

Triple Seizure

It came again, fresh meat within its jaws,
attempting, with a dripping mouth, to rob
me of the summer-soft serenity.
All afternoon I smelled that breath on me,
hot tongues of fire unsettling my repose.
Not one, not two, but triplets this time clamped
and held on tightly, would not let me go.
I tried to rest from each renewed attack,
but monsters don't tell time. Another smack
slammed harder. Then, exhausted, I fell back,
completely swallowed, Jill to Jonah's Jack.

It Strikes Again

Three bolts of lightning suddenly arrive
within my vehicle and try to drive.
I wake one quiet Thursday afternoon
to blood-red streaming suns of deep maroon.
My foggy brain will not cooperate,
and I need someone else to advocate.
My 20/20 vision has gone blind.
What once was tied up tight has now untwined.
The irony of seizure's strange assault
reminds me: These events are not my fault.

Elusive the Answer

I seek an answer to the question: Why
me? Why have seizures struck and won't let go?
I ask, but silence echoes its reply.

The day begins, a graceful butterfly,
but soon I feel the strength of undertow
and can no longer even wonder why.

I do not have a choice but to comply
when sparks of neural storms cause vertigo.
I beg, "Please, no," to silence's reply.

As if a devil punched me in the eye,
I reel, kicked far from castle to Skid Row.
Where is the answer to my question? Why,

electric charges, do you crucify
all normal functions, steal the status quo?
I ask, but silence echoes its reply.

When seizures dwell in me they occupy
cerebral fields, and I must shovel snow
to unearth answers and to find out why
the haunting echoes silence their reply.

Brain Fire

The doctors talk of neurons firing fast,
reporting conflagration in my head.
The blaze begins, and part of me has fled
to distant lands, exploding like a blast

from outer into inner space, harassed
as if my mind is uninhabited.
A frozen stillness holds me as I'm led
through languid hours. How long will this ice last?

Last night a seizure's strength hit, unsurpassed.
Today, molasses-slow and thick, I tread
in struggle through the underbrush I dread.
The flames of this brain burning flabbergast
me, soon die down. The smoldering coals, still red,
subside, yet leave me once again aghast.

Dark Waters

Resurfacing awake between the past
and now, a mix of voices jangles. Vast
the distance between sound and meaning. Words
bounce everywhere. I try to hold those birds
that wing away. Will I forever stay
immobilized of mind, no hope of May
or June, July? Thick terror slices thin
my sleep wherein I dream a javelin
impales my struggling neurons. Clock hands creep.
Sharks circle menacingly through the deep.

Jail

My sudden silence sends me to a hell,
dark land of unfamiliarity.
I do not recognize the clientele

in this place where my name scratched on a cell
etches its emphasis. Captivity
locks me in sudden silence, in a hell

that you can never enter. Now I dwell
where others chart the course. An absentee,
I do not recognize the clientele

here. No kind voice helps me to bid farewell
to all my dreams. This odd complexity
of sudden silence sends me to a hell.

Again, tense tangled neurons cast their spell.
My brain dispatches a hostility
I do not recognize. The clientele

stands at my bed and rings a clanging bell.
I wrest away from its grim prophecy.
My sudden silence sent me to a hell.
I blench to recognize its clientele.

Arrival of the Ambulance

Two strangers in our bedroom talk to me,
but I am far away and do not hear.
I lie in foggy ambiguity.

The arms of seizure grip this refugee
while ambulance attendants now appear,
two strangers in our bedroom. "Talk to me,"

they urge. I hear, but my ability
to speak has vanished. Locked in wretched fear,
I lie in foggy ambiguity.

A small space in my mind knows burglary
has been committed. What would commandeer
me? Now I hear two strangers. "Talk to me."

Tranquility turns into tyranny
when grand mal seizure dares to interfere.
I lie in foggy ambiguity.

Intrusions in my equanimity
provoke me like a high-seas mutineer.
As strangers in our bedroom talk to me,
I lie in foggy ambiguity.

Metaphors for Seizure:
An Anaphora

When mental locomotives jump the track,
when hours decelerate in daytime's black,
when wrecking ball turns mansion to a shack,
when land beneath my feet feels earthquake's crack,
    the threat of seizure strikes.

When pistons in my brain screech to a stop,
when I can't tell the bottom from the top,
when drought kills all the fields of withering crop,
when Times Square New Year's Eve ball will not drop,
    the threat of seizure strikes.

When harmony blurs to a monotone,
when Mozart's melodies become a drone,
when I can't tell a stripe from herringbone,
when I lie in a hospital alone,
    the threat of seizure strikes.

When fires of creativity burn down,
when I can't hear the noises of the town,
when colors of the rainbow all turn brown,
when Queen Elizabeth has lost her crown,
    the threat of seizure strikes.

When shadow monsters chase around my bed,
when hammers pummel thoughts within my head,
when deep within I feel a sense of dread,
when I don't hear what anyone has said
    and threat of seizure strikes,

I inch away from their horrendous blow,
so savage are the actors in this show.

Medical Leave

Again I'm isolated, jailed away
in tightened rooms, dark, damp and subterrene.
Meanwhile worlds spin and universes play.

The colors in the box have all gone gray,
although I wish for rose, aquamarine.
Again I'm isolated, jailed away,

remembering the joys of yesterday.
O, how I'd rather be a peregrine.
Meanwhile worlds spin and universes play

a thousand light years from my present fray.
Like measled child I suffer quarantine
again. I'm isolated, jailed away,

and others hold the magic key, the say
about when, how, or if to intervene.
Meanwhile worlds spin and universes play.

They move in circles that revolve. I stay
in limbo, queen of all that's unforeseen.
Again I'm isolated, jailed away
from worlds that spin, from universe's play.

My Car

The law in my state dictates that a driver must not drive for six months after an epileptic seizure. I am in the second of these periods within seven months.

It sits unmoving in the driveway dead
when I would rather make it charge ahead.
Convulsions take my license well away.
With it I see my freedom ricochet.
I learn the turtle's lesson, slow my pace,
plunge once again into this fearful place.
All day and night the threat of seizure lives
within my head, becomes thick narratives.
I wish I could obliterate this plot.
Now, though, I feel the tightness of the knot.

Fine Line:
Part One

Horizon splits the day from night. I watch
as dark devours its light – a bite – then tints
of shiny hours remain reflected in
the sky. Pink tracings summon memory.
How quickly present fades, becomes the past,
requiring that I do a sudden flip.
My eyes adjust to dark, but always dance
a slight step slower than the night's advance.

When entering such darkness, walls enclose
me. Halls of mauve and gray pretend a cheer.
Soon disappearing, blurs of color bend
into a motionless array. Where are
the trees I used to see when passing by
this way? They've rotted from the inside out
and left me nothing but a shadow. Gone
again the lovely shades of living green.

Adjusting to the dark is trickery
not visual alone. The hunter, pulsed
determination stirring in his blood,
sets traps intently, treads to wooded blind,
awaits the opportunity to find
his mark. A teeming forest sickens with
the shotgun blast. Escapees all, but how
much longer can the graceful deer run scared?

Fine Line:
Part Two

Imprisoned in a bed, dependent on
a nurse to whisper by, I cry. Unknowns
familiarize themselves, an odd torment.
Whose voices speak? Reality's been rent.
I knock on doors to find what I once knew,
but hear, repeatedly, "And who are you?"
A deadbolt tightens the assault, its thud
a dull and final lock, a gagging halt.

With military discipline it plagues
me, staunch in its attack, the battleground
a bloodied tangle recently renewed
from ravages of war. Pursuers gain
in speed and strength. I stumble all alone
across the land, poor competition for
the army massed and trained for my defeat.
The spoils of war, however, *will* be mine.

The unpredictability of war
annihilates my peace. A line's been drawn
between advancing soldiers and the dove.
They march, determined for the victory.
With vengeance, enemies now crest the hill...
then change into a sudden, sullen camp.
No one is there. Aghast, they stare into
the dust where someone's boot erased the line.

Fine Line:
Part Three

Now all has quieted again. My mind
replays events which, in the recent past,
obliterated peace. Confusion reigned
for one short time, my days a hastily-
tossed hand of jacks. No pattern could predict
eventual design. Each scattered piece
fell into its position, rearranged,
a jigsaw, ground and sky each in its place.

The mornings offer fright, uncertainty:
Are demons crouching just behind my door?
Do I possess the strength for one day more
of battle? Now, relentless, I pursue
whatever's there and pull out all the stops,
release artillery, stand sentinel
at all the posts. Without surrendering,
I diligently guard inheritance.

The slender line is etched as if on glass,
a ballerina-pointe partitioning.
I pause, considering the opposites
inhabiting each side of delicate
incision. Who's to say which way I'll fall?
A poise precisely balances my form
while I breathe carefully, respecting each
place on the other side of one fine line.

Numbers

The therapeutic range of one of the anticonvulsant medications
I take is between 10 and 20. I am most healthy when a blood-
level test shows a number close to the middle of that range.

> The numbers need to swim within mid-range
> to keep me floating far from seizure's grip.
> I can't risk high or low that might estrange
> me from myself or sink my battleship.
> To sail the waves, fourteen is fine, ten's not.
> How delicate the dance, this regimen
> that poises me within my Camelot.
> The oarlock in my boat has come undone
> so, paddling, I get nowhere on this sea.
> Wild seething waters drown me, whirling brew
> unleashing neurological debris
> that drenches consciousness. How that storm blew.
>
> When numbers rise or fall out of their range
> the neurons in my brain cannot count change.

Tiger

I hear the tiger prowling in my brain,
awakening from winter where it has lain
asleep. Its stirrings throw the switch and slow
my circuits, empty my portfolio.
Awake, the heavy-footed jungle beast
assails me, then enjoys its neuro-feast.
Without a care it shreds my consciousness
just like the moths that chew right through my dress.
I am a tree uprooted from its ground,
tornado-tossed and wildly thrown around.
The animal again escapes its cage.
What can I do to barricade its rage?

New York and Me

My brain, like towers that exploded, fell
into itself, and crumbled into ash.
I heard the deathly soundings of a knell.

Strong girders, beams and stairs now parallel
the ground, and one great city looks like trash.
My brain, like towers that exploded, fell.

The Towers and my mind have fought to quell
devouring blazes warning of a crash.
We both heard deathly soundings of a knell,

collapsed before the strength that would propel
us down the flaming stairs. Fires seethe. Limbs thrash.
My brain, like towers that exploded, fell.

Now crafty devils fling me to their hell.
Thousands of victims in the Towers dash
about, attempting to escape the knell.

I recognize my hollowed, emptied shell,
hear echoes whistle. Where's my mental cache?
Like those exploding towers, my brain fell
prey to the deathly soundings of a knell.

War

My neural soldiers lie in disarray,
thoughts shredded, tangled, and awareness stilled.
Upon the battlefield I'm cast away,
and live in neuro-winter, frozen, chilled.

Thoughts shredded, tangled, and awareness stilled
shadow my sights. Now shrouds of blooded sun
send me to neuro-winter, frozen, chilled,
hold hands with me in deep oblivion.

My shadowed sight, shrouded by blooded sun,
bequeaths to me its crazy legacy,
holds hands with me in deep oblivion.
I dread the permanence of injury.

This world bequeaths its crazy legacy.
Upon the battlefield I'm cast away,
dreading the permanence of injury,
my soldiers once again in disarray.

Symptoms

You might not see what I so strongly feel:
A labored fight each day to hide, conceal
the seizure symptoms. Slippery as an eel,

they slide from well-sewn pockets into sight.
A flat fatigue and speech impairment might
lock me in limbo. Taunting, they invite

me to their chambers, show me my new room.
With broken consciousness I now presume
they reign as bosses in this frightful tomb.

A numbing silence keeps me company.
I look, but cannot find, a rescue key.
Repeating seizures, with a frequency

as regular as seasons, execute
attacks upon my weakened brain. Recruit
the jury, give me strength to prosecute.

Awakening, slow, dull, an uphill climb
awaits. Confused and out of touch, meantime,
I try for normal. What a pantomime.

Another tally mark against my name
totes up the damages. What nasty game
was played on me? I work hard to reclaim

pre-seizure self, but all remains a blur.
On some strange ship I sailed as passenger.
When pulling into port, an officer

gave his permission that I disembark.
I find it difficult to see through dark,
and fear again the lurking, hungry shark.

Tonic-Clonic Seizure

This trail departs into a wilderness,
the neurons of my brain in overdrive.
All words have jettisoned this poetess.

As I become awake, start to assess
the wreckages of seizure, I revive.
This trail departs into a wilderness,

a frightening place of wide unruliness.
With might I try to call them back. I strive,
but words have jettisoned this poetess.

I lie in hollow halls, lie comfortless,
while others care and know I will survive.
This trail departs into a wilderness.

A demon wrangled me, mean, merciless.
I want to write my thanks that I'm alive,
but words have jettisoned this poetess.

Words usually make me rich. Now penniless,
I'll wait for old friends to again arrive.
This trail departs into a wilderness
where words have left me a mute poetess.

Weather Changes

I hardly notice, when the days are green,
the effortlessness of my working brain
until discharging power turns the scene

from blossoms to a blizzard. Crashing train-
wreck stills my engines, spills the priceless oil
that lubricates my wheels. Tons of it drain

like rain from clouds. No matter how I roil
against my now-obstructed mind, I fail,
and fall into a hinterland. Black soil

absorbs me like a thirsty man whose stale
parched throat gulps water. Mindless wanderings
lead me down lonely trails. Cyclonic gale

whirls me to unseen lands and madly brings
unrest to broken brain. It apprehends,
and tightly captures me. Now seizure kings

of underworlds reign. Their power sends
my sense to nether places far away.
I give up self-control to strangers. Friends

come to my side but I can't even say
hello. I see their doubt. They agonize
in silence. Dangling strings the color gray

define my wounded brain. I mobilize
against the warrior, but cannot root out
this epileptic plant of beanstalk size.

Earthquake

You shake your finger in my face and laugh.
Erratic, unpredictable, you bat
me to a seven on the seismograph.

I am a stranger in this paragraph
where rhythms of the rolling words fall flat.
You shake your finger at me, laugh your laugh,

rip through the middle of my photograph.
I beg you, don't turn up the thermostat
on me. At seven on the seismograph,

my flag hangs temporarily half-staff
as I negotiate this habitat.
You still shake fingers in my face and laugh,

vain vandals of my brain. My epigraph
engraves its words but will not tip its hat
to earthquake's seven on the seismograph.

I cannot grasp the pen to autograph
your page until I tame this jungle cat.
Stop shaking fingers in my face. Don't laugh.
Soon coming? Zero on the seismograph.

Gift Wrap

"I wrap them differently," God said to me
of gifts. "The paper doesn't always shine.
Mysterious My ways, don't you agree?

I rose from crude and ugly gallows tree,
dying of thirst, was given gall for wine.
I wrap them differently," God said to me.

Yes, I must learn He would not guarantee
a perfect life, that dark and light combine.
Mysterious His ways, don't you agree?

"My child, reflect upon Gethsemane.
See how I made death's enterprise divine?
I wrap them differently," God said. To me,

a package should be pleasing, a trustee
of elegant surprise that waits within.
Mysterious His ways, don't you agree?

When seizure strikes, the gift-wrap warranty
expires, requires my pen to countersign
the gifts wrapped differently. God said to me,
"Mysterious My ways. Don't you agree?"

Part Three:

RECOVERY

Decrescendo

In spiraling from quick to slow
I fall into adagio,

and as I plunge through fright ahead
into the pitch-black night of dread,

the maestro lifts his hands and halts
the crazy rhythm of this waltz.

I cannot know how long it takes,
but soon my injured brain awakes

and notices the tempo changed,
the score rewritten, rearranged.

Electroencephalogram

I wonder what this beeping robot tells
the doctor of me: Beethoven and how
I play his Pathetique? New status, now
a grandma? How I love a chocolate cake?
Son uniformed policeman, daughter first-
rate mom? The differences in children's lives
because I teach? Emotions wobbling as
my mother passes from this life? The warmth
of husband's care in circumstances bleak?
The pen records brain energy as lines
that peak and fall from pasted probes which serve
as conduit from my most precious place.

I wonder what this beeping robot tells
the doctor of me. Does he now know more?

An Old Town

A winding spiral staircase leads me down
past stores now boarded-up, the old downtown
a shadow of its former self. The slum
exists on hope, and dirty glass makes glum
the faces of the passersby who cry,
"Restore what we cannot identify."
And I, awakening from seizure's grip,
know well, and feel confining censorship.
Will others see me as I was before
the blight, or through their tightened smiles ignore
me? Oh, the once-proud city aches. Disgrace
climbed over porches. I tried to erase
the terror seizure spreads. An architect
begins again, removes the disrespect,
and with his pencil draws a brand-new plan.
Where squalor sat, now blooming gardens ran
along grand boulevards. The cornerstone
of this fine town was nearly overthrown
by sudden floods. New buildings, sidewalks, parks
surround this epileptic. She remarks,
"I'll sparkle in my renaissance. Come, please,
walk through, and see me thankful, on my knees."

Seizure

The men who run around inside my brain
conduct but cannot stop this speeding train.
They punch my ticket, grin their secret grin,
        as terrorists now suddenly unpin
all knots, loose what was so securely tied.
Malicious, mean and smug, self-satisfied,
        they list me in their book of refugees,
        refuse to offer me apologies.
Holding the pen, I guide each sentence clean,
        words economical and phrases lean.
I paid the price asked by this train's cashier,
        but I know who remains the engineer.

Storytelling

The trails of my fine brain wind endlessly,
invisible to eye, yes, held from sight,
its many stories my biography.

How temporal the lobe of mastery.
Please, for my earth time, kindly expedite
the trails of my fine brain. Wind endlessly

throughout my myriad activity.
I give you rapt attention as you write
my many stories, a biography

comparing integrated harmony
with splits of all that needs to reunite.
The trails of my fine brain wind endlessly,

reintroducing capability.
The epileptic brain longs to recite
its many stories. My biography

has changed and, granted now an amnesty,
acknowledges the shiftings of the night.
The trails of my fine brain wind endlessly
across my stories, my biography.

Time Travel

It's been five freedom years since seizure last
tossed sticks of dynamite into my brain.
I move in careful moments from the blast,

and wake long after dew has dried, amassed
its nectar from the cup of grass, maintain
these five fine freedom years. Since seizure last

pronounced that it would never be outclassed,
my strong resolve created a campaign
to move in careful moments from the blast.

Tight tangled yarns unraveled while a cast
of limitation offered me a cane.
It's been five freedom years since seizure last

controlled me in its grasp. Now slow, not fast,
I join the class that learns the gift of pain,
and move in careful moments from the blast.

I traveled eerie streets, but finally passed
through fear. True north blows on the weather vane.
Within these freedom years seizures don't last,
but care must always guide me from the blast.

Resting

I rest now from assailants of my brain.
You thought you won. I watch you from afar.
What breathless scenery in this terrain.

No longer does a seizure's dread refrain
send invitations to your seminar.
I rest now from assailants of my brain.

Go where you wish. In stuffy closets reign
with your enormous power so strange, bizarre.
What scenery engraves my new terrain

where mountains raise their arms and entertain
my senses. Here I feast on caviar.
I rest now from assailants of my brain.

Was I just helpless Abel to your Cain?
No longer vassal to a mighty czar,
I revel in my rearranged terrain

and toast it with a goblet of champagne.
My triumph parallels a shooting star.
For now I rest. Assailants of my brain,
don't dare disturb me in my new terrain.

Cracked Mirror

In hands of others I have now become
a different person, my identity
insidiously changed. You'd recognize
this twin, yet now I wear a coat that *they*
have sewn. I hear, in seizure's aftermath,
their hushed and whispered voices: "...sick again."
That makes me cringe. I want to shed, like snakes
their skins, acquaintance with the charge that I'm
a woman who laid down her head. Instead,
please lift me back from temporary hell
with resurrection words. I want to dwell
with you, the living. I can do it well.

My Family during Seizure

Although it's day, a hand draws curtains past
my eyes, and sudden certain dark arrives.
A buttered yellow day turns overcast.

Adrift and clouded, unaware of blast,
I sleep while others feel the slash of knives.
Although it's day, a hand draws curtains past

my family as they seek the sun, but vast
impending blackout interrupts their lives.
A buttered yellow day turns overcast.

The hours between convulsions – still, steadfast –
draw stomachs into knots. The nightmare thrives,
although it's day. A hand draws curtains past

the recent radiant light. The two contrast,
blind night, day's hope, yet confidence revives
the buttered yellow day once overcast.

The weatherman's prediction – ha! – won't last.
In spite of grand mal seizure, health survives.
Again it's day. A hand draws curtains past
that buttered yellow day turned overcast.

Brain Storm

Parietal and temporal, occipital,
the lobes of my brain occupying inner space
mean little to me, seem alas, quite commonplace...
until they run into a seizure's obstacle.
And then the humming of the parts, that miracle,
grinds to a stop. The lobes no longer interlace.
Meantime, I spend long hours, a captive in this place
while neurons strain to organize within my skull.

Time drags me through a broken consciousness, and days
delay when I can once again know my own name.
Return will not be hurried, and the fog remains.
My brain moves slowly, agonizingly, through haze,
ongoing Herculean efforts to reclaim
the beauty of this land before the hurricanes.

Coming Out of Seizure

The landscapes come again into my sight,
and magnified, new focus brings them clear.
Small boy with candle, as my acolyte,

do not let seizure's criminals incite
my justice as it tries to commandeer
those landscapes. Come again into my sight,

calm lakes, majestic mountains. Please invite
me to your parties. I'm no longer mere,
small. Boy with candle, be my acolyte,

directing me from darkness. Reunite
me with earth's harmonies and hear me cheer
the landscapes. Come again. Please, to my sight

bring all my former favorite feasts despite
a seizure's strong attempt to interfere.
Small boy, you have become my acolyte.

This brain sometimes misfires like dynamite
that causes consciousness to disappear.
But landscapes come again into my sight.
I thank you for your candle, acolyte.

Looking Ahead

I've had no seizures in a year or two.
Hot bolts of lightning challenged me to fight,
but now they fade. Relieved, I bid adieu

to fiery furnaces that I once knew,
the flames extinguished and burned out of sight.
I've had no seizures in a year or two.

The neurons in my brain make their debut
in rhythms regular as day and night.
As seizures fade away I bid adieu

to terrifying shadows. Well-to-do,
I climb Mount Everest. Health holds me tight.
I've had no seizures in a year or two.

I traveled on a twisted avenue,
gulped down by seizure's greedy appetite…
But now that fades away. I bid adieu

in celebration. Oh, this rendezvous,
this balm of Gilead that sets things right.
I've had no seizures in a year or two.
They fade, and with relief I bid adieu.

Proclamation

2010: No seizures to announce.
No disappearances into the dark.
Locked in its cage the monster cannot pounce.
I breathe a little easier. So stark

the differences between cerebral life
and silence where sound fades to monotone.
Remembering the terror and the strife,
I sigh. The enemy is overthrown.

A seizure is a Sunday with no bell
to ring in hope. I grope through dark instead.
That hides now in the past, and I rebel
against relentless captors while I tread

the grassy fields, the mountains, sandy lanes.
These pictures light up possibility.
I see the landscape through new windowpanes.
Cerebral jail doors open. I am free.

Puzzle Pieces

Arrange the pieces, fit them into forms
to make a whole. Keep out the thunderstorms.
When I awake from seizure's compromise,
I beg my brain to please apologize
for causing chaos. Kleptomaniac,
it ransacks ordered patterns and makes slack
the supple shape of brain. Through eerie night
the puzzle pieces repossess the light
of consciousness. I'd like to buttonhole
each mental piece, but I have lost control.

Tension

A seizure, absolute in strategy,
taunts me with unpredictability.

Denied

I thought I'd make a list of what has been denied:
An autumn weekend gathering of college friends,
    a get-together with enormous dividends.
They walked the beach while I, unconscious, slept inside

a room of fear. One year I missed all Christmastide.
    Awaiting family to enjoy gifts, dinner, cake,
    an aura sneered at me. *No, don't make me forsake
this time.* But seizure had its way, pushed me aside

again. I had no choice but to relent. The slide
    into that hollow hole took melodies and words,
    my favorite J.P. Sousa marches. Golden thirds
turned dissonant, and now I felt my mind divide.

Wait! Listing things that epilepsy took from me
is like unscrewing bulbs that light up my marquee.

Questionings

"Who is this?" someone asked. I didn't know
my husband's name or recognize his face.
"When were you born?" *What's wrong? Why can't I show
this nurse how information lost its place?*

Bright shots of lightning split the trees, then spit
their twigs and branches toward the leaden sky.
When seizure wrecks my day I must submit
to all its weapons aimed at me deadeye.

My nervous system has one trillion cells,
and seizure shatters them like fragile shells.

Day after Day

Between my seizures life goes on as planned
as if no interruption ever breaks
the rhythm. Like an hourglass spilling sand

it moves me in its flow without demand,
makes constant progress like the little flakes.
Between my seizures life goes on. As planned,

I climb my mountains, glory in the grand
and soothing singing lullabies of lakes,
the rhythm like an hourglass spilling sand

until...electric charges, out of hand,
disrupt the flow. I hear those screeching brakes.
A seizure interrupts the life I'd planned.

Dependable old systems have been banned,
but now each day away from seizure takes
the rhythm like an hourglass. Spilling sand

reminds me, in its whisper, of command
for celebration, thanks, and candled cakes.
Between my seizures life goes on as planned,
the rhythm like an hourglass spilling sand.

Sleep

I love to stay up late to read a book
or talk with longtime friend as night hours wane.
But I need sleep and can no longer look
past midnight or a seizure might arraign
my brain. This epilepsy's grabbing hook
uproots the trees upon my hill and plain,
sets hours for sleep, dictates what I can cook,
consume, and do. Hear me: I WANT FREE REIN!

A Step Higher

Give me another day that does not seize,
a day without the fury of a seize.
I am collecting them, hypotheses

to prove they might become my battle song,
yes, one upon another, battle song
as I go out into the world, head strong.

The storm of neurons flung me well outside
of normal function, flung me well outside,
cut power to my mind, and terrified

me. Now I turn my face and bid farewell.
In stronger voice I speak my firm farewell.
No longer seizure's victim, I can dwell

upon a higher ground. Renewed, my mind
leaves all debris of winter far behind.

A Note to You

Do you know anyone with this disease?
Would you continue to be patient, please?
Because of medication we pay fees
for free and flowing conversation. Ease

throughout a day does not belong to us.
No, often we remain anonymous.
Dark shrouds of clouds hang low, not cumulus.
We fear the grappling arms of octopus.

Each day we gird ourselves against these foes
as clanking iron neuro-gates foreclose
on us. We wish our poems and our prose
took us someplace where freedom never froze.

A Hope

A seizure ends, a curl of consciousness
returns. I see dark disappear. Now light
illuminates my forward steps to bless
me with good health. No longer dim, but bright,

    my life kicks once again into high gear.
I watch the shark retreat to waters deep,
the monster find another hemisphere.
My fingers cross that they remain asleep.

Afterword

Although I have been seizure-free now for five years, I am reminded that a seizure can strike at any time for any reason. Even when I do everything right in terms of being compliant with my medications, getting enough sleep, eating well, avoiding caffeine, and managing stress, a seizure can still occur. The most predictable part of epilepsy, I have found, is its sheer unpredictability.

I hope that you have found some comfort in reading my poems. My greater hope is for your health.